The Revelations of

Saint Bridget of Sweden
(1303-1373)

Book 11: "The Sermon of the Angel"
Book 12: "Four Prayers
Plus
The Fifteen "Magnificent Prayers of Saint Bridget"
to Our Suffering Lord Jesus Christ

Edited by Darrell Wright, 2018

CONTENTS
The Revelations of St Bridget of Sweden

1. Book 11: "The Sermon of the Angel": On Salvation History from Adam to Christ

Chapter 1   Sunday – First Reading
Chapter 2   Sunday – Second Reading
Chapter 3   Sunday – Third Reading
Chapter 4   Monday – First Reading
Chapter 5   Monday – Second Reading
Chapter 6   Monday – Third Reading
Chapter 7   Tuesday – First Reading
Chapter 8   Tuesday – Second Reading
Chapter 9   Tuesday – Third Reading
Chapter 10 Wednesday – First Reading
Chapter 11 Wednesday – Second Reading
Chapter 12 Wednesday – Third Reading
Chapter 13 Thursday – First Reading
Chapter 14 Thursday – Second Reading
Chapter 15 Thursday – Third Reading
Chapter 16 Friday – First Reading
Chapter 17 Friday – Second Reading
Chapter 18 Friday – Third Reading
Chapter 19 Saturday – First Reading
Chapter 20 Saturday – Second Reading
Chapter 21 Saturday – Third Reading

2. Book 12: "Four Prayers"

Prayer 1
In this prayer revealed by God to blessed Bridget, the glorious Virgin Mary is devoutly and beautifully praised for her holy conception and infancy, for all her virtuous acts and labors, for the great sorrows of her whole life, for her most holy death and assumption, etc.

Prayer 2
This prayer was revealed by God to blessed Bridget. In it, by means of a painstakingly detailed narrative, Christ is beautifully and devoutly praised for His glorious incarnation; for all the actions, labors, and sorrows of His life and of His holy death; for His ascension into heaven; for the sending of the Holy Spirit upon the disciples, etc.

Prayer 3
In this prayer, revealed by God to blessed Bridget, praise is given in a beautiful way to all the members of the most holy body of our Lord Jesus Christ and to His body's most virtuous actions.

Prayer 4
In this prayer, which was divinely revealed to blessed Bridget, most devout and beautiful praise is given to all the members of the glorious body of the Virgin Mary and to all her body's virtuous actions.

3. THE FIFTEEN PRAYERS OF SAINT BRIDGET TO OUR SUFFERING LORD JESUS CHRIST

1. Book 11: "The Sermon of the Angel": On Salvation History from Adam to Christ

Chapter 1
Sunday – First Reading

When John in his Gospel speaks of the Word, that is, He who is, and has ever been, with the Father and the Holy Spirit, one God, in this one God, there are truly Three Persons, yet not three Gods, for in the Three Persons is only one divinity, the one, perfect Godhead, belonging equally to each; and in the Three Persons, only one will, one wisdom, one power, one beauty, one strength, one love, one joy.

The Word, then, being for ever one with the Father and the Holy Spirit, is truly God. A familiar word like *one* can help us, perhaps, to understand – for each of the three letters is necessary to the whole, and we cannot take away one letter without destroying the meaning. So in God, there must ever be the Three Persons, equal in all things, with all things equally in each, for there can be no dividing of God. There was no dividing when the Word, the Son of God, took a human nature; He was not separated, by this, from the Father and the Holy Spirit. He took our human nature, yet remained ever the Word of God. His human nature was necessary for Him, to achieve our salvation. It can help us to understand this if we consider how our thoughts and our words are not things we can see or touch, except in so far as writing gives them a more material existence.

The Word of God, the Son of God, could not have come as one of us, or lived with us, for our salvation, unless He had taken on our human nature. A written word can be seen and read, then understood, then spoken. The Son of God can be seen, in that flesh He took to Himself, and so we can understand and have no doubt that He is one with the Father and the Holy Spirit. Truly then, there are Three Persons, undivided, unchanging and unchangeable, eternally in all things equal, Three, yet but one God. Since God is eternal and timeless, all things were eternally known to Him, before their existence in time.

Then, when He willed them to be, they came to be with that exact perfection which suited their purpose. The divine wisdom of God willed all things to be what they are for His own honor and glory. He had no need of them; it was not to make up for any deficiency in Himself – something wanting to His goodness or joy – there can be no defect or deficiency in God. It was His love, and His love alone, which led Him to create; that there might be beings, apart from Himself, whose existence should be an existence of joy, deriving from His own being and joy. All things, then, foreseen by God, and present to Him eternally, though as yet uncreated, had already that design and perfection which they would possess when His creating brought them to be.

One thing excelled all others, designed and perfected by God with a special joy. This was Mary, the Virgin who was a Mother, the Mother who was ever a Virgin.

It has been said that all created things are made up of four elements – fire, air, water and earth. If so, then in Mary's pure body these elements were to have a special perfection: the air should be fittingly an image of the Holy Spirit; the earth should be rich and fruitful, for the growth of useful things, to supply every need; the water should be calm and non-threatening, unruffled by every wind; and the fire so strong and bright that all the earth should be warmed by it, and the heavens themselves.

Virgin Mary, we know that in you the design and perfection willed by God have come to be. As He foresaw you, so He has perfectly created you. And of all His creation, you please Him most. The Father rejoiced that He would do so much through you: the Son rejoiced in your holiness and love: the Holy Spirit rejoiced in your lowliness and obedience. The Father's joy is that of the Son and the Holy Spirit: the Son's joy is that of the Father and Spirit: and the Holy Spirit's joy is that of the Father and the Son.

Father, Son and Holy Spirit rejoice in you, the one joy of Three who are One. Father, Son and Holy Spirit love you, Mary, the love of the Three Persons, One God.

Book 11 – Chapter 2
Sunday – Second Reading

Mary, we know that you were ever in the mind of God, before His creating brought you to be – the most perfect of all His creatures. He knew you as Noah, before the flood, knew the Ark he was to build, and the way he was to build it. The design of the Ark had been made known to him, and he waited for the time when God would command him to set to work. The design and perfection, Mary, of your glorious body, the Ark of God, was known to God before all time. And He knew the time when He would bring it into being by His creating. As Noah rejoiced at the thought of the Ark he was to build, so God rejoiced, Mary, at the thought of you. Noah's Ark would withstand the storms; you, Mary, the Ark of

God, would withstand, in the strength of your holiness, every attack of the hatred and sin of hell.

Noah's Ark was so built that no water could seep in – a ship whose timbers were carefully protected both inside and out. You, Mary, the Ark of God, would be so strong in God's grace, anointed and protected by His Holy Spirit, that no desire would ever enter your heart, either for your own glory or for the possession of earthly things. Such desires, we know, are as displeasing to God as the water which seeps into the keel of a ship, and collecting there becomes state and offensive.

Noah was pleased at the size and capacity of His Ark. God rejoiced, Mary, in that holiness which would be yours, in your love which would embrace all creatures, and in your gentleness which would look with pity on sinners, and hate only what was hateful to Him. But most of all, He rejoiced in that ever increasing grace which would fit you to bear in your womb that which heaven and earth could not contain, the Person of God the Son, to hold Him and be truly His Mother.

Noah took pride, as every captain of a ship takes pride, in the cleanliness and tidiness and brightness of the Ark. God rejoiced, Mary, in your virginity, for in you there would be no sin, nor slightest stain of sin, to taint your perfection. Noah provided for himself and those with him, all that was needed to survive the days ahead. God chose you, Mary, for His Son, that your body should provide for Him a perfect human body. Noah came from the Ark unchanged. But from you, Mary, the Ark of God, the Son of God came forth, clothed with that pure flesh and blood which He had taken from you.

When Noah left the Ark, its purpose was served – it was empty and useless. But when Christ came forth from your womb, you were filled with every gift of the Holy Spirit, growing ever in holiness, not further now from Christ, but nearer to Him, and dearer even than before, united to Him on earth and in heaven for ever.

Book 11 – Chapter 3
Sunday – Third Reading

From the moment of God's promise, through the long years of waiting, Abraham loved the son who was to be his, the child who would be called Isaac. How much more did God love you, Virgin Mary, whom He had foreseen from eternity, and knew before your creating, for He knew also the joy your birth would be to Him. Abraham did not know how his love for God would be tested and proved through his promised son.

But God knew with His divine knowledge how through you, Mary, His great love for man would be made known. Abraham knew that Isaac would be born of his union with Sarah, a child conceived unexpectedly in their old age. God knew that His Son would be conceived in you, Virgin Mary, without the intervention of man, and be born of you, true Mother yet ever a Virgin. Abraham knew that his son once conceived would grow without his help to become a person, independent of his father. God knew that the sacred body of His Son, formed in your womb, would in a special way, be for ever most intimately united with the Godhead. This must be so, since the Son is ever in the Father, the Father in the Son, equal yet one.

Abraham knew that he and his son must return to dust in the corruption of death. God would not allow your pure body, Mary, to see corruption, for it was the flesh and blood of your body which had been given to form the body of His Son. Abraham built a house for the son who was to be born to him. But God Himself, the Blessed Trinity, is the dwelling in which you, Mary, will abide for ever. In a wonderful way, then, your dwelling, Mary, was in God, who surrounded you with His protecting love. Yet God dwelt ever in you, leading you to the highest holiness by His presence. For his promised son, Abraham prepared wheat, wine and oil, three kinds of essential nourishment.

For you, Virgin Mary, God Himself was to be your eternal meal, Father, Son and Holy Spirit, Three yet One. And through you He was to give Himself to men as the food of life. So we may attribute this food of life in a way, to you, Mary, since it is by you that it has come to us. The three things which Abraham prepared can be thought of as a sign of the action of the Three Persons. Oil cannot burn without a wick. This can suggest to us That the love of God the Father could not be made known on earth without the humanity of the Son, that humanity which He took from you, His Virgin Mother.

Wheat was to be made into flour, and then bread, for our daily use. The Son of God, though He is truly the food of Angels, could not be our food without that flesh and blood which He took from your loving womb. Wine cannot refresh us unless it is in something we can drink from. The Holy Spirit could not be poured out upon us without the humanity of your Son. For the salvation which Christ's Passion and Death accomplished is the fount of all the delights and graces bestowed by God on Angels and on men.

Book 11 – Chapter 4
Monday – First Reading

It was love that led God to create. There could be nothing lacking in God, nothing wanting to His goodness or His joy.

It was out of love alone that He willed creation, that there might be beings, apart from Himself, who would partake of His infinite goodness and joy. So the Angels came to be, created by God in countless numbers. To them He gave free will, freedom to act, in accordance with their nature, as they willed. As He Himself is under no necessity but has created out of love alone, He willed that the Angels, whom He designed for eternal happiness with Him, should likewise be under no necessity. He looked for love in response to His love, obedience to His offer of eternal joy.

Yet in the first moment of their creation, there were Angels who chose, freely and deliberately against their Creator, in spite of His infinite love, which called them to love in return. Justly they fell, fixed in their evil will, from an eternal joy into an eternal misery. But not all fell. To those Angels who chose love for love, there was given the contemplation of God in all His glory, power and holiness. From this contemplation, they came to know the eternity of God, that He has no beginning and no end; they learned what it meant to have Him for their Creator; and they saw most clearly how everything they possessed had come to them from His love and His power.

They learned too that His wisdom had given them a wisdom of their own, but which He allowed them to foresee the future. And it was a joy and consolation to them to know that God in His mercy and love wished to replace, in His own way, those Angels who had forfeited by pride and envy their place in heaven.

In their contemplation of God, the Angels saw with wonder a throne placed next to that of God Himself. They knew that the one for whom this throne had been prepared had not yet been created. Yet already they loved this chosen one, and rejoiced as they waited. Their love for each other was born of their love for God. But between these two loves they saw one who was more lovable than themselves, one whom God loves with great joy more than all His creatures. Virgin Mary, you were the chosen one, destined for that throne near to the throne of God.

It was you whom the Angels loved, after God, from the first moment of their creation, seeing in the contemplation of God, how beautiful He had made themselves, but how much more beautiful He would make you. They saw that in you there would be a love and a joy far greater than their own. They saw too the crown that awaited you, a crown of glory and beauty surpassed only by the majesty of God. They knew how God their Creator was glorified by themselves and they rejoiced. They knew how much more He would be glorified by you, and they rejoiced still more. Before ever you were created, Mary, God and Angels together rejoiced in you.

BOOK 11 – CHAPTER 5
MONDAY – SECOND READING

God's creation of the world and all it contains took place in the instant of His will's expression; and with that design and perfection foreseen by Him. Yet there remained still uncreated another work of creation which would surpass what He had already done. You, Mary, are, as it were, another world, a world which God foresaw with greater joy, a world the Angels were more pleased to contemplate, a world of more benefit to those of good will that the whole earth and all it contains.

Mary, we may see in God's act of creation and in all created things an image of your creating. We read that it pleased God to separate the darkness from the light when He created the earth. How much more it pleased Him to enlighten you from childhood. The darkness, the time of your infancy, was made light by your knowledge of God, your understanding of God, and the will to love for God which day by day led you on to a love surpassed only by the love of God.

The mental darkness of childhood, without knowledge of God, without reasoning power to guide, is for us a time of defenselessness and danger. But we know that for you, exempt from sin, it was a time of purest innocence. We read that it pleased God to make, together with the stars, two lights – the sun for daytime, the moon for the night. It pleased God still more, Mary, to set in you two heavenly lights, brighter and more beautiful than the sun or the moon: the first – perfect obedience, a radiant light for Angels and men to admire, guiding all who saw it to God Himself, who is the light of eternal day; the second – a most complete and trusting faith, the light to men in the darkness of despair and unbelief when your Son chose suffering and death, a light to cast out all shadow of doubt and uncertainty when He rose from the dead. We read that it pleased God to create the stars. The thoughts of your heart, Mary, were more pleasing to Him.

We read that it pleased God to create the birds, whose flight and song are a delight to men. All the words which you spoke, Mary, heard also in heaven to the joy of the Angels, were more pleasing still. We read that God created the earth itself, the dry land and the soul; and flowering and fruit-bearing trees of many kinds. Your life, Mary, your occupations and work, were more pleasing to Him, for you would give nourishment, and life itself, to all, and your love would make each act of your life more beautiful to God and the Angels than the fairest of flowers are to men. God created the plants, flowers, trees, and fruits, minerals, metals, and precious stones – He has made the earth rich with these things.

Yet He saw in you, Mary, even before your creating, more qualities and virtues than in all earthly things. We read that God's creation was pleasing to Him, and that He looked with joy on all He had done. It pleased Him still more to create you, Mary, and He looked with greater joy on you, even before your creating, than on this earth and all earthly things. That world and everything in it, – all would be destroyed. Though created before you, Mary, it would not endure. But you, by God's eternal decree, were created to be for ever, and to be for ever united to Him in deepest love, created in fullest grace, responding to His grace in all things, and so growing to the perfection of holiness.

BOOK 11 – CHAPTER 6
MONDAY – THIRD READING

God is the Creator of all beings, and He is Being itself. Nothing can be or come to be without God. Therefore, this world and all things in it owe their existence to Him alone. He is the Creator of all. And Creator, last of all, of Man. To mankind He gave, as He had given to the Angels, the gift of free will. He wished that be free choice man would cling to what was good, and so avoid a just punishment and earn a just reward. Among men, little regard is paid to work done unwillingly, under threat of punishment.

We honor work done willingly out of love, and it is such work that deserves reward. It pleased God rather to leave them free, making known what a reward obedience would win, and what punishment pride and disobedience would incur. God created man, forming him from the dust of the earth. He looked for man's love and obedient service, that so the places of those Angels who had disobeyed in their pride, and fallen from joy into misery, might be filled once more. They should have received a crown of joy for their love and obedience. Instead, they lost their reward, hating not only the joy they had forfeited but also those virtues which would have assured it to them.

A king is given a crown of gold, calling all to honor him who wears it. But there is a heavenly crown for each virtue, calling even to men on earth to honor one who loves God, calling to Angels in heaven to rejoice, calling to God to reward. What of the crown of God Himself? In Him all virtues reside, surpassing in every way every other possible good. In Him all is virtue. Yet three special virtues stand out in what we know of God, three crowns of incomparable glory. First, that He created the Angels. (It was the envy of such glory that led some of them into their pride and fall.) Second, that He created Man. (The loss of God's glory was man's most grievous loss, when in his folly he let himself be led into sin.) Third, that He created you, Virgin Mary.

The fall of Angels and of man did not lessen the virtue of God, or take from His crown of glory. They were created for God's honor, and they refused it, it is true, just as they were created for their own desire, and yet forfeited it by sin. The wisdom of God turned their sin into an even greater glory for Himself. For your creation, Mary, gave such glory to God, that what was refused Him by Angels and men was made good a thousand times over. Virgin Mary, our Queen and our hope of salvation, you may truly be called the crown of God's honor. Through you He showed His divine virtue.

From you He won honor and glory greater than from all other creatures. The Angels knew, even before your creating, that by your holiness and humility you would overcome the pride of the Devil and his hatred for man. They had seen how man had fallen into misery, but in their contemplation of God, they still rejoiced, knowing well what great things God would do, Mary, through your lowliness, when His creating brought you to be.

Book 11 – Chapter 7
Tuesday – First Reading

We read in the Bible of Adam's original state of happiness. Then of his disobedience to God, which brought so much suffering and sorrow. We are not told that he continued in disobedience. From his conduct after Cain had killed Abel, his refraining from intercourse with Eve until he knew that this was no longer the will of God, we may judge that the love and service of God was his first thought. His sorrow was not so much the unhappiness he had brought on himself, but rather the offense he had committed against God.

Created by God, owing his existence and his happiness to God, he had turned against God, and so justly deserved God's anger. This was true sorrow, bringing with it repentance and humility. And with this true sorrow came also consolation from God. One thing, and one thing only, could have fully consoled him – the promise that God Himself should come as man, of Adam's own race, and by love and humility redeem that race which his pride had deprived of life.

That God should be born as men are born was unthinkable. Adam and Eve owed their beginning in some way to a special creation by God. Even this would not be fitting for the coming of God to earth. It would seem that Adam understood from God's words something of what was to be. At least, we may picture him foreseeing the future, foreseeing a woman, like Eve in womanhood, but lovelier and holier than all of his race, a virgin and mother, bringing God Himself to this world. We may think of him grieving at the words spoken to Eve by the Devil.

But rejoicing, his sorrow turned to joy, at the thought, Mary, of your words to the Angel. We may think of him grieving that Eve his wife, created by God from his body, had deceived him and drawn him on to eternal death. But rejoicing that you, Virgin Mary, would bear in all purity Christ, the Son of God, to restore man to life. Grieving that Eve's first act was of disobedience; rejoicing that you, Mary, would be a daughter of God, most dear to Him in all things, ever obedient to His will.

Grieving that Eve had been tempted, in the sight of God and all the Angels, by the false promise of being made like to God; rejoicing that in the sight of God and the Angels, you, Mary, would acknowledge yourself the Handmaid of God. Grieving that Eve had offended God, and brought about the condemnation of man; rejoicing that your word to God should bring such joy to yourself and to all men. Grieving that Eve had closed to man the gate of heaven; rejoicing that your word had opened that gate again to yourself and to all who sought to enter. So we may think of Adam rejoicing with great joy at the thought, Mary, of your coming, as we know the Angels rejoiced, before the creation of the world, foreseeing your creation by God.

Book 11 – Chapter 8
Tuesday – Second Reading

Adam's punishment made him see the justice and mercy of God. Throughout his life he feared to offend God and was guided in all things by love for God. This way of life he handed on to those who came after him. With time they forgot God's justice and mercy. With time they forgot God Himself, and that

He was their Creator. They believed only what pleased them, immersing themselves in pleasure and sin.

So came the flood, when God destroyed all men on earth, saving only Noah and those with him in the Ark, through whom He willed to people the earth again. Once again men multiplied on the earth, and once again they fell, tempted away from God, turning to the worship of false gods and idols. God's mercy and fatherly love led Him to intervene, and He chose one who was a faithful follower of His law, Abraham, to make a covenant with him and his descendants. He fulfilled his desire for a son, and Isaac was born. And He promised that from his descendants, Christ, His son, would come.

It is possible that Abraham, by God's permission, foresaw many things. We may think of Him as having foreseen Mary, the Mother of Christ. We may think of Him rejoicing in her, and loving her more than Isaac his son.

It was not greed or ambition that led Abraham to acquire lands and wealth. It was not for his own sake that he desired a son. He was like a gardener of some great lord's estate. He had planted a vine, and planned to make cuttings from that vine, and so in time make for his master a vineyard of great worth. Like a good gardener, he knew that each plant needed careful attention, and proper feeding, if it was to bear good fruit. One plant in particular he cherished, watching its growth with great delight. He knew that it would be the choicest of all the trees in his vineyard.

His master would love to rest in the shade beneath it, praising its beauty and the sweetness of its fruit. If Abraham was the gardener, then the vine which he first planted was Isaac; the cuttings of that vine his descendants; the feeding of each plant the goods of this world which Abraham acquired for the sake of Isaac and his race; the most cherished tree, that tree of beauty and sweetness, was the Virgin Mary; and the Master for whom Abraham the gardener worked, the owner of the vineyard, was God Himself, who waited till the vineyard (the race of Isaac) was established, and then, coming, saw with content, the perfect vine in the midst of His vineyard, the Virgin Mother of God. The beauty of this tree was the perfect and sinless life of Mary; the sweetness of the fruit, the acts of her life; the shade of that tree, her virginal womb, overshadowed by the Spirit of God.

If Abraham then foresaw what was to be, he rejoiced in his many descendants, but most of all in that one of his descendants who, as Virgin Mother, was to bear the Son of God. This faith and holy desire Abraham handed on to Isaac, his son: your oath, he had said to the servant sent for Isaac's wife, must be sworn on the One who is to come of my race. Isaac too handed on this same faith and desire, when he blessed his son Jacob.

And Jacob in blessing his twelve sons, handed on this same faith and desire in his turn to Judah. God so loved Mary, the Mother of His Son, even before the creation of the world, and before her creating, that He gave to those He had specially chosen as His friends some foreknowledge of her, for their consolation. First to the Angels, then to Adam, and then to the Patriarchs, the creation of Mary was a thing of wonder and joy.

BOOK 11 – CHAPTER 9
TUESDAY – THIRD READING

God is all love, and all loving; infinite in love, and infinite in loving. We may truly say – God is love. He makes known His love to those who love, and all things speak to them of the love of God. See how great was His love for His People, the People of Israel. He delivered them from the Egyptians, and led them out from captivity, into a fruitful land, that they might live there in peace and prosperity. It was this prosperity that was envied by the Devil, and in his hatred for all that was loved by God, he tempted God's People, and by his deceits, led them time and again into sin.

They had the Law of Moses; they were the People whom God had made His own, through His covenant with Abraham; yet they fell into idolatry and worshiped false gods. God looked on them and found there among them some who still served Him with true faith and love, following His law. To strengthen these followers of His, amid the dangers that surrounded them, to confirm them in their faith and love, He raised up among them the Prophets, men who came not only for the help of God's own, but also to rescue those who had made themselves enemies of God.

In time, like the mountain streams which join, and then join to other streams as they descend, increasing ever in volume and power, carrying all before them, down at last to meet other waters and in the lower lands form into the great rivers, the Holy Spirit filled the hearts of His Prophets, and first one, then another, then more raised their voices, to speak as He inspired them, till their sound filled the ears of many, to comfort and console, to call back and restore. The sweetest sound of their voices was that news of joy – that God Himself would be born of a Virgin, to make amends for the evil which Satan, through

Adam, had caused to man; that He would redeem man, and rescue him from his misery, restoring to him eternal life.

Joy too, that God the Father so willed this redemption of man that He would not spare even His only-begotten Son: that the Son so willed to obey the Father, that He would take to Himself our human flesh: that the Holy Spirit, though inseparable from the Father, willed to be sent by the Son. The Prophets knew that the Son of God would come into this world, to be light in our darkness, brighter than the sun at dawn, to proclaim God's justice and love. But they knew He would not come unheralded. As the morning star heralds the sun, they foresaw that a star would rise in Israel, fairest of all the stars, in brightness and beauty surpassed only by the sun itself. This star with the Virgin Mary, who would be Mother of Christ, her love surpassed only by the love of God, her heart ever responding to the will of God.

This news was given by God to His Prophets, to console them in their labor of teaching, and encourage them in their trials. For they grieved at the pride and sinfulness of the People, who neglected the Law of Moses, rejected God's love, and incurred His anger. But they rejoiced, Mary, in you, foreseeing that God, that giver of all law, would receive back to His grace those who had sinned, for the sake of your humility and holiness of life. They grieved to see the Temple empty and desolate, and the worship of God neglected.

They rejoiced, Mary, to foresee the creation of that holy temple, your pure body, where God Himself would love to reside. They grieved at the destruction of the gates and the walls of the holy city, broken by armies, invaded by sin. They rejoiced, Mary, to foresee how you would stand firm, against all attack, a strong citadel where Christ would arm Himself, the gate through which He would come forth to His conflict with the Devil and His own. To the Prophets, as to the Patriarchs, your coming, Mary, was a thing of wonder and joy.

BOOK 11 – CHAPTER 10
WEDNESDAY – FIRST READING

Before God made known His law to Moses, man had to live without a rule of life. Those who loved God, did what they thought was God's will. Those who rejected His love, and did not fear to do so, acted as they chose. To dispel their ignorance, God in His goodness made known His law, teaching first the love of God, then love for others, then His will concerning marriage, its holiness and binding force, its purpose in His plan – the growth of His people. The union of man and woman in a holy marriage was most pleasing to God, for He willed to choose the child of such a union as the Mother of Christ. The eagle, flying above the earth, looks down at the trees, and choosing with its sharp eyes the tallest tree, one firmly rooted to withstand the storms, one that cannot be climbed, one that nothing can fall on, builds there its next, God sees, with penetrating gaze, all things, both present and future.

He looked therefore among all men and women, from the beginning to the end of time, for a husband and wife fit for the bearing of the child of His choice. He found none so worthy as Joachim and Anne, who lived together in holiness and a love for each other born of their love for Him. It was to them He entrusted the one who was to be Mother of His Son. She was to be, as it were, the eagle's nest, in which He could find protection and shelter. Joachim and Anne were the tall tree in which this nest would be built, firmly rooted in a union based on the love and honor of God; the branches of this tree their lifelong thought for the will of God, and their desire for a child, not for their own sake, but to beget one who would grow to love God and serve Him as they themselves did.

The tallness of this tree, beyond the reach of the winds, and higher than all around, was the height of holiness which Joachim and Anne had attained, beyond the attacks of Satan, untroubled, except by the thought that God's honor was many times assailed by the sins of many, with no thought of honor or worldly possessions, no pride or ambition to move them from their selfless love of God.

God knew that for the birth of the Mother of Christ, none holier could be found than Joachim and Anne. What a treasure you held, blessed Anne, while she who was to be Mother of God rested in your womb. How precious to God that seed of Mary's life in your womb, more precious than the offspring of all men on earth. Anne became God's treasure-house, keeping safe this most precious thing, this seed of so precious a life.

God saw it and watched over it, for as His Son was to say – where one's treasure is, there is one's heart. The Angels looked on this treasure with joy, knowing how precious it was to God their Creator. It was a holy and blessed day, to be honored by all, the day when this precious seed was first sown. God Himself and the Angels greeted that day with great rejoicing.

BOOK 11 – CHAPTER 11
WEDNESDAY – SECOND READING

That seed of life was ready, and at God's chosen moment, life began as He infused into it a living soul. We see the bees in summer, busy making flowers for honey; led by instinct to their sweetness, they seem often to wait for the buds to open. God foresaw, as He foresees all things, the birth of Mary, and He waited with joy as she lay hidden in her mother's womb, for He knew that none ever of those to be born would equal her in holiness. None would so make known to men His infinite love.

The infusing of Mary's soul in the womb of Blessed Anne was more beautiful than the dawn of the most beautiful day. As we so often long for the dawn, so Angels and men longed for her birth. Where the nights are short in summer, so that there is little darkness, people do not notice the dawn; they wait for the sun itself, thinking of their crops and their fruits. Where the nights are quite long, even in summer, the dawn is watched for and welcomed, not only for the coming of the sun to the fields, but because men weary of the night and the darkness.

The Angels in heaven did not await the coming of Mary that they might see Christ, for they were ever in the light of His presence; they longed for her, so that the love of God might be made known in the world, so that men who loved God might be strengthened in their love, and then they, the Angels, could go out to gather them as an everlasting harvest for God. But men, living in this world of sorrow and hardship, desired the coming of Mary that they might see Christ their Savior. They longed for her coming, that they might learn from her perfect life how man should live. The Virgin Mary is foretold as the branch which would grow from the root of the father of David, to bear a flower on which the Spirit of God would rest. In her mother's womb – how light Anne's burden! – Mary was the tender branch which would soon come forth. The flower that branch would bear was Christ.

He Himself, from the moment of her assent to God's message, was a richer and infinitely sweeter nourishment than blessed Anne had given to her. Though Mary was to Him the food of life, giving her own flesh and blood to be His, that He might appear in true humanity, He was to Mary her heavenly food, that she might bear Him as her child, though He was truly the Son of God. They were Mother and Son, Son and Mother, yet this Son was truly the Son of God, the only-begotten Son of the Father, eternally with Him, eternally united with Him and the Holy Spirit, eternally the Person of the Son of God, who with the Father and the Spirit lives in glory, eternally One.

BOOK 11 – CHAPTER 12
WEDNESDAY – THIRD READING

In Father, Son and Holy Ghost, there is only the one Divinity. There is ever the one divine will. A fire with three flames is but the one fire. The three flames of love in God are the one love of His will, burning to fulfill His one divine purpose. The love of the Father was seen most brightly by the Angels when they knew His will to give His Son for the redemption of man. The love of the Son proceeding from the Father was seen most brightly when the Son willed to deprive Himself of His glory and take the form of a slave.

The love of the Holy Spirit was seen most brightly in that readiness to make known in many ways the one will of the Three. All heaven was ablaze with these flames of God's love, to the delight of the Angels. Yet all heaven must wait; must wait for the coming of Mary. The redemption of man, willed and foreseen by God, could not take place without her. A flame of divine love was to be kindled in Mary which would rise up to God and return so filled with His love that no corner of this world would be left cold and in darkness.

When Mary was born, she was like a new lamp, all ready to be lit; to be lit by God with a light burning like the three-fold flame of His own love. The first flame of her lover was her choice, for God's glory, to be ever a virgin. So pleasing was this to the Father that He willed to entrust to her His beloved Son, that Son who is inseparable from the Divinity of Himself and the Holy Spirit. The second flame of her love was her humility, so pleasing to the Son that He willed to take from her a true human body, and that humanity which was destined to be honored in heaven above all things. The third flame of her love was her obedience, which brought to her from the Holy Spirit the fullness of grace.

It is true that these flames of Mary's love were not lit at the moment of her birth. She was still, as other children, only a little one, unaware of God's will. Yet God took more pleasure in her than in all other beings. She was like a sweet-sounding harp, not yet in tune; but He whose treasure she was knew how lovely the music He would make with her.

It may be believed that Christ's knowledge was not lacking in anything due when He was conceived in Mary's womb. We may believe too that Mary developed in understanding earlier than others. Since the coming of Mary was such joy to God and the Angels, men too must rejoice, and give glory and honor to God, who chose her from all His creation by eternal decree and willed that she should be born among sinners, to bring forth in sinlessness the Savior of the world.

Book 11 – Chapter 13
Thursday – First Reading

Speaking of the beauty of Mary, we think of lovely things: her sacred body is like a vase of purest crystal; her soul like a lantern of clearest light; her mind like a fountain of water rising up into the air, then falling in cool streams to the deep valley. Passing from infancy to childhood, to the age when she was able to understand, she began to think of the existence of God, and how He made all things, and especially man, for His own eternal glory, and how His justice embraces all things.

Her thoughts reached out to God, as the waters of the fountain rise into the air; then, like those waters flowing down to the valley, her thoughts returned to herself and brought her a most profound humility. The Church sings of Christ leaving and returning to the Father, though He was ever with the Father and the Father ever with Him. Mary's thoughts reached up to heaven in contemplation and grasped God by faith. Then in the love with which God possessed her, she turned her mind again to God and to herself, never losing her thought of God. Together with hope and trust, and with holy fear, the fire of this love inflamed her heart, as the flame is the brightness of the lantern.

She understood the perfect subjection of body to soul, and no discord ever troubled her, so that in body she was purer than purest crystal. How soon she learned to appreciate God's love, and treasure it with all her being! Think of this love as a lily which God had planted, with a threefold root, bearing three flowers of great beauty. The three roots are three most powerful virtues, protecting her body. The three flowers, three adornments of her soul, which gave great joy to God and the Angels.

The first of the three virtues was her abstinence, her right use of God's gifts of food and drink – no over-indulgence to make her slow in the service of God, no unwise austerity to impair her health. The second was her wakefulness, so that she rested no longer than was necessary – not wasting God's time in laziness, but not fatiguing herself to the detriment of her work. The third was her command over her will, so that she was not easily wearied in body, and never over-anxious or over-excited.

The first adornment of her soul was her love for the things of God rather than the things of earth, no matter how beautiful these might seem to be. The things men so often prize, possessions and wealth, were utterly distasteful to her. The second adornment was her appreciation of the infinite distance between worldly honors and spiritual glory. This world's praises were as abhorrent to her as the poisoning air of corruption. The third adornment was her love for all that God loves, her repugnance for all that was hateful and displeasing to Him. She sought in all things the true sweetness of God, and no taste of bitterness was permitted to endure in her after her death.

With such beauty of soul, Mary surpassed all other created things. God willed that only through her should His promise be fulfilled. Her love left no blemish or defect, not even the smallest. In nothing could the enemy claim victory over her. If then she was so pleasing in the sight of God and the Angels, may we not think that she had also great earthly beauty? Those who saw her looked with delight, and knew that her loveliness was born of her love for God. They saw her, and loved to see her, and were led to a new love for God.

They watched her, and loved to be with her, and knew that no evil could touch them, nothing sinful attract them, in the presence of her beauty and holiness.

Book 11 – Chapter 14
Thursday – Second Reading

With our slow and clouded minds, it is hard for us to appreciate that moment when Mary first knew God and gave herself to Him. His will became her one desire and her joy. She saw how she owed everything to His creating; but she knew that according to His plan, her will was free, to choose or refuse His will and His way. She saw the blessings which God had already bestowed, and for these alone she chose to love Him in return, and to love Him for ever.

Soon she was to understand how much more He would do, She learned that He who created all would not rest content, but would Himself come to His creation as redeemer of His creatures. And this out of love alone. She learned that man's will, free to choose good or evil, could make satisfaction to God for sin, or incur His anger by sin. In that moment of understanding, she chose once for all her course through life.

The captain of a ship knows what dangers lie ahead, and he charts his voyage to avoid the storms. He watches the ship's course, and works out the distance sailed, and the distance still to sail before arriving in port. Every rope, every piece of equipment is in place and ready for use. The cargo he carries must reach port as quickly as possible. Every detail of the voyage must be worked out ahead. Mary was like the captain of a ship.

As soon as she had understood God's will, she set her course according to His commandments. She was watchful at all times that her attention should never be distracted from God. She took care, when those around her spoke of their ambitions, their successes or failures, not to let herself become less devout in her service of God. Anything contrary to God's law she knew at once as a danger to be avoided at all cost.

With this self-training and discipline, all that she did was good. All that she said, all that she listened to, all that she gave her attention to, was sensible and wise.

Her work was useful to herself and to others, and each journey she made had some good reason. The trials of life she accepted with patience and joy. Her one thought was God. Her one desire was to be for ever with Him, to offer to Him in return for all He had done for her all her love and her praise. So perfect a life won her from God, who is the giver of all good things, the highest holiness and glory. It is no wonder that God lover her more than all other creatures.

She alone of all men and women was ever sinless and immune from sin. How near she was to heaven at that moment when the Angel Gabriel greeted her – Hail, full of grace! How pure, how holy she was, at that moment when the Father entrusted to her His only Son, at her assenting – Be it done unto me, according to thy word! At that moment of time, Divinity was united with humanity, humanity with Divinity; the Son of God was made man; the Son of the Father become the Son of Mary.

BOOK 11 – CHAPTER 15
THURSDAY – THIRD READING

This union between God and man, between Christ and the Virgin Mary, only God can comprehend. The Son of God, truly God, all present and present to all, whose eternal dwelling in heaven is the Blessed Trinity itself, made for Himself on earth a dwelling-place in the womb of the Virgin Mary. The Holy Spirit, who is ever in the Father and in the Son, rested in Mary, filling her, both body and soul, with His presence. The Son, who is ever with the Father and the Holy Spirit in heaven, acquired for Himself as man a new dwelling on earth. The Father too, with the Holy Spirit, dwelt in a new way on earth, in the humanity of the Son, for the Father with the Holy Spirit must be ever in the Son. The Son alone took flesh.

He alone took our humanity. True God, He came as man to men, withholding from the eyes of men His Divinity seen ever by the Angels in heaven. All who hold the true faith must rejoice unceasingly at this union achieved through Mary. The Son of God took in her womb true flesh and blood, and true humanity, not losing His Divinity: in divinity was humanity, in humanity Divinity. Christ did not lose His Divinity, nor Mary her virginity.

It would be utterly wrong to think that God could not have done such a thing, for all things are possible to God. It would be equally wrong to think that He would not have done such a thing for His own, for this would deny the goodness of God. If we believe then that God could and would do such a thing, why do not all men love God with all their love?

Picture some king, honored by all, with great power and possessions, and someone dear to him suffering great insult and injury; if the king took on himself the burden of his friend, if he gave all his wealth to save him from poverty, still more, if he offered his life for his friend, would not this be the greatest love he could show? But no love of men on earth could equal the love of God in heaven. No love could equal that love which led God to condescend to our need, and entrust himself to the womb of the Virgin Mary and take there our humanity.

Mary is like that bush which Moses saw, burning yet never consumed by the fire. God Himself was there, till Moses knew and obeyed His word. And to him He made known His name – I am who am, the name of the eternal. The Son of God dwelt in Mary, till the span of time between conception and birth was completed. At conception, He had taken, by His Divinity, full possession of Mary's pure body. At birth He came forth, with His Divinity united for ever to true humanity. But as the sweet perfume of the rose leaves the rose still as lovely, His coming forth was no lessening, but truly a glorification of the virginity of Mary.

To God, to the Angels, to Adam, to the Patriarchs and the Prophets, and to countless servants of God, this Burning Bush, which was Mary, brought joy beyond words – Mary, in the fire of her love, conceiving the Son of God – the Son of God in obedience to the Father, resting in her, to be born, true man, true God, of a Mother and Virgin, a Virgin-Mother. To ourselves also, and to all our race, this must bring great rejoicing and consolation. The Son of God, He who with the Father and the Spirit is the eternal God, has taken our humanity, through the love of the Virgin Mary.

Her love embraces all things that belong to God. We then may claim, and be sure of her intercession. We can say truly than man who deserved eternal death through sin can acquire eternal life only through her. From Mary, the Son of God came in perfect humanity, to fight as man with Satan who had subjugated man. To Mary, men must resort for strength against Satan's temptations. Mary is the gateway by which Christ entered into this world, to open to man the gate of heaven. Pray then, pray then to Mary, that at death she may come to us, to secure for us entry into the eternal kingdom of Christ, her Son.

BOOK 11 – CHAPTER 16
FRIDAY – FIRST READING

We are told that Mary was afraid when the Angel appeared and spoke to her. It was not fear of any bodily harm to herself, but dismay at the thought that this might be a trick of Satan, to lead her into sin. At the moment when her mind first knew God and His holy will, she had chosen for herself a life of love, and this brought with it a wise and holy fear of God.

It is our delight to call Mary a rose of great beauty. We know that the lovelier and healthier the rose, the stronger and sharper are the thorns which surround it. It Mary is a rose of beauty, she will not be untouched by the sharp thorns or trial and sorrow. Indeed, as the days of her life went by, her sorrows increased in bitterness and pressed more heavily upon her. Her first sorrow was that fear of God which her knowledge of His existence and His will had brought her. It was a sorrow to her that in all she did, she must keep in mind the thought and threat of sin. She directed each thought, word and work to God, but there was always the fear that some defect might creep in to lessen its value in His eyes. How foolish are those who deliberately and without fear throw themselves into all kinds of sin, bringing on themselves suffering and sorrow.

Mary was sinless, and immune from sin. Everything she did pleased God. In every way she was entirely pleasing to Him. Yet she never allowed herself to be free from the fear of displeasing Him. A greater sorrow still was in her heart, for she knew from the writings of the Prophets that God willed to come as man, and suffer as man. In her love for God, this caused her great grief, though she did not yet know that she was to be the Mother of God. When that moment arrived, the moment when she knew that the Son of God had become her Son, to take in her womb that human body which was to suffer as the Prophets had foretold – who could measure her joy?

Who could measure her sorrow? Like the rose, she had grown in beauty, but the thorns had grown too, stronger and sharper and more piercing. To Mary it was joy beyond words that her son should come in humility to lead man to heaven, saving him from the penalty which Adam's pride had incurred, the misery of hell. It was great sorrow that the sin of Adam by which man rebelled in both body and soul should require the redeeming death of her Son in such agony of body and soul.

It was great joy to her to conceive her Son in sinlessness and purity. It was great sorrow to her that this so loved son was born to suffer a shameful death, and that she herself would be there to stand and see. Great joy to know that He would rise from death, and win in return for His Passion an everlasting honor and glory; great sorrow to know that this glory would not be won except by the agony and shame of the Cross. The perfect rose blooms in beauty on its stem, and our delight is not spoiled by the sharp thorns around it.

The sharp thorns of Mary's sorrow piercing her heart could not change her or weaken her will, and in her suffering she accepted whatever God's will should demand of her. We call her a Rose of Jericho, for men say that nowhere can so lovely a rose be found. In her holiness, Mary is more beautiful than all mankind, surpassed only by her Son. To God and the Angels in heaven, her patience and willing endurance brought joy. To all on earth, it must be a joy to meditate on her sufferings so willingly accepted, and on that consolation she had ever in her heart, that all was the will of God.

BOOK 11 – CHAPTER 17
FRIDAY – SECOND READING

The Prophets foretold many things about Christ. They spoke of the death of the Innocent One and the pains He would suffer to win for men on earth an eternal life with Him in heaven. They foretold and set in writing that the Son of God, to save all men, would be bound, scourged, mocked, led out to be crucified, and reviled as He hung on the Cross. They knew that the immortal God would take man's mortal form. They knew that He willed to suffer as man for man.

If the Prophets foresaw these things, would not Mary foresee them, even more clearly? She was the Mother predestined for the Son of God. How could she not have foreseen His sufferings when He took flesh in her womb for this very purpose? The presence of the Holy Spirit would enlighten her, so that she knew better than the Prophets that things which they, through the Holy Spirit, foretold.

At the moment of Christ's birth, as she held Him for the first time in her arms, Mary foresaw the fulfillment of prophecy. As she wrapped Him in swaddling-clothes, she foresaw the scourging of His flesh which would make Him a leper in the eyes of men. The hands and feet of her Child brought the thought of the nails which would pierce them. The face of her Son, beautiful beyond the beauty of men, was the face men would spit on. His cheeks would feel the blows of their hatred. His ears would hear the curses of their defiance.

His eyes would be blinded by the blood from the wounds in His head. His mouth would taste the bitterness of gall. His arms would be bound, then stretched in agony on the Cross; and His heart, empty at last of blood, would shrink in death. No part of that sacred body would escape the bitterness of that most bitter death. And when all breathing ceased, there would still be the soldier's sharp spear to pierce His lifeless heart. Mary rejoiced as no mother ever rejoiced when her Son, the Son of God, was born, true God, true man, mortal in His humanity, immortal in His Divinity.

But Mary knew sorrow deeper than the sorrows of all mothers, foreseeing the Passion of her Son. Her joy was beyond words, but her joy brought with it a sorrow deeper than all the sorrows of this world.

A mother's joy is complete when her child is born and she sees it healthy and perfectly formed. Her pain and anxiety are over. Mary rejoiced at Christ's birth, but she knew that no moment of her life would be free of sorrow. The Prophets foretold, long before the coming of Christ, His sufferings and death. Simeon foretold, in the presence of Mary and her Child, the piercing of her heart by a sword of sorrow. We know that the mind is more sensitive to pain even than the body.

We know that the soul of Mary, even before the death of her Son, would feel that sword of sorrow more sharply than all women on earth would feel the suffering of childbearing. Each day brought nearer the sufferings of Christ. Each day brought nearer the piercing of Mary's heart. It was the compassion of Christ alone which enabled her, by His presence and His words, to bear day by day such piercing sorrow.

Book 11 – Chapter 18
Friday – Third Reading

You shall seek me and shall not find me'. These words of Christ were the sharp point of the sword of sorrow, entering Mary's heart. That sword pierced deeper at the betrayal of Judas, and at the arrest of Christ, when He willed to be taken by the enemies of justice and truth. Deeper still at each insult offered to Christ, with each suffering inflicted on Him. The sorrow of her heart overflowed into all the members of her body. She saw how cruelly Christ was struck, and more cruelly beaten and scourged. She heard the sentence of death passed by the Jews. She heard the cries of the people – Crucify him, away with him!

She saw Him led out, bound as a criminal, to a traitor's death. She saw Him struggling to carry His Cross, dragged forward and whipped as He stumbled, led like some wild beast rather than a lamb to the slaughter. As Isaiah had foretold, He went meekly to His death; like the lamb that is led to the slaughter house, like the sheep that is dumb before its shearers.

Christ was patient in His sufferings. Mary endured patiently the sorrow of His sufferings. She followed Him, even to the place of death. She saw the wounds of His scourging, the crown of thorns, His cheeks disfigured with blows, His face covered with blood, and she wept in sorrow.

She saw Him stretched on the Cross, and heard the blows of the hammer as the nails pierced His hands and feet. So great was her suffering and sorrow that her strength almost failed her as she stood by and watched. She saw the vinegar and gall offered for His lips to taste. and her own lips could not move in prayer. She heard His cry – My God, My God, why hast thou forsaken me?, and saw His head fall forward and His body become rigid as He breathed forth His spirit. She stood and saw how He died. Then truly was her heart quite pierced by the sword of sorrow. It was the strength God gave that alone saved her from dying in such sorrow. To see her Son, stripped and bleeding, dying, pierced by a lance, mocked by those who stood by, jeered at by soldiers, deserted by all but a few of His chosen ones, abandoned by so many whom He had won to justice and truth, to see this most bitter death – could there be sorrow so deep as her?

We read that once, when the Ark of God fell into the hands of enemies, the wife of one of God's priests died for sorrow. How much greater was the sorrow of Mary, for she saw the body of her Son, which the Ark prefigured, nailed to the wood of the Cross. Her love for her Son was love for the Son of God, greater than the loves of all men. If the loss of the Ark could cause sorrow and death, the death of Christ would have brought Mary to death but for God's gift to support so grievous a sorrow. By His death, Christ opened the gateway to heaven, and won for His own their entry into joy. Mary looked up from the depths of her sorrow, as one coming back from the gates of death.

Her faith never faltered that Christ would rise again, and in this faith she could comfort many whose faith had failed. They took Him down from the Cross, and wrapped Him in fine linen with spices, and laid Him in the tomb. Then all left. Few still had faith that He would rise. Little by little, the sorrows of Mary's heart lightened, and she felt the first sweetness of consolation. The sufferings of her Son were at an end. She knew that on the third day He would rise, would rise with His humanity united again to His Divinity, would rise to everlasting honor and glory, to suffer, to die no more.

Book 11 – Chapter 19
Saturday – First Reading

We read that the Queen of Sheba made the long journey from her own lands in the south to visit Solomon the King. Her journey was not wasted, for she found great delight in His words. No gifts were too precious for her to give, no praise too high, and she departed in admiration of such great wisdom. The Virgin Mary spent long hours in thought, considering the course of events in this world, and all the things that this world holds dear. Nothing delighted or attracted her, except the wisdom she had learned from God. This was her desire and her search, and she did not rest till she had found it in Christ.

In the Son of God she found wisdom infinitely greater than Solomon's. The Queen of Sheba was overcome with wonder as she contemplated the wisdom of Solomon. Mary was overcome with sorrow as she pondered the loving wisdom of Christ, who saw salvation in suffering, and willed to save man from subjection to Satan by His sufferings and cross. When at last the sufferings of Christ were over, Mary looked up from the depths of her sorrow, ever offering herself and her will to God for His glory, gifts most precious to Him. Gifts too of another kind, for many were led to the truth of God by her faith.

No words or works of men were so powerful to bring men to God. Many lost faith when they saw Christ die. She alone withstood the unbelief of men, seeing in Christ her Son the Son of God, over whose Godhead death could have no dominion.

When the third day came, it brought bewilderment and anxiety to the Disciples. The women going to the tomb to anoint the body of Jesus sought Him and could not find Him. The Apostles were gathered together in their fear, guarding the doors. Then, surely, though we are not told of this in the Gospels, Mary spoke of the resurrection of her Son, that He had truly risen from death, that He was alive again in all His humanity, no more subject to death, risen to an eternal glory. We read that Mary Magdalen and the Apostles were first to see the risen Christ. But we may believe that Mary His Mother knew of His rising before all others, and that she was the first to see Him.

It was Mary in her lowliness who first gave praise and adoration to the risen Christ. When Christ ascended to the glory of His kingdom, the Virgin Mary remained on earth. We cannot know what her presence meant to so many. Those who loved God were strengthened in their love; those who had turned from Him were brought back to His love. The Apostles looked to her for guidance and counsel. The Martyrs found in her, courage to face suffering and death. The Confessors of the Faith were strengthened in their believing. Virgins were drawn to her purity. Widows were consoled by her sorrows. Husbands and wives found in her a pattern of perfection. All who heard and obeyed the word of God found in Mary great comfort and help.

Whenever the Apostles came to her, she was able to teach them about Christ, and help them to understand. The Martyrs rejoiced to suffer for Christ, for He had suffered for all. They remembered the long years of sorrow borne so patiently by Mary His Mother, and they bore their martyrdom even more readily. The Confessors, meditating on Mary, learned many things about the truths of the Faith. From her example, they learned too the wise use of earthly things, food, drink and sleep, work and rest.

And how to order their lives in all things to the honor and glory of God. Virgins learned from Mary's example true chastity in virtue. They learned too the wise use of their time, how to avoid vanity and foolish talk, and see all things in the light of true holiness. Widows learned from her consolation in sorrow, strength against temptation, and humble submission to God's will. With a mother's love, Mary could never have wished for the death of her Son, still less for the death of the Son of God. Yet she willed in all things the will of God. She chose for God's sake the humble acceptance of suffering and sorrow.

Husbands and wives learned from Mary true love for each other, in body and in soul, and the union of their wills, as of their flesh, in all that the will of God demanded. They learned how she had united herself for ever with God by faith, and never in any way shown resistance to His divine will.

BOOK 11 – CHAPTER 20
SATURDAY – SECOND READING

We read in the Gospels these words of Christ – the measure you give shall be the measure you receive. No one on earth can know the glory of Mary, the Mother of God. She who on earth gave so much receives now in heaven a measure of glory beyond the whole of creation. When it pleased Christ to call her from this earth, there awaited her all whom her holiness had helped. God Himself, whose love had been made known only through her, awaited her coming to adorn her with a glory surpassed only by His own. She was raised to the highest place in heaven, to be Queen, not only of His earthly creation, but Queen over the Angels for ever.

The Angels rejoiced in this Queen, made for ever obedient to her by their love for her. Those Angels too who had fallen from God were made subject to her; not temptation of theirs could withstand her; no one calling with love for her help would be left unprotected; the tempters would choose rather an increase of their misery than the opposing of her power. Of all creatures the most humble, Mary is now the most glorious, the most perfect in beauty, and nearest to God Himself. As gold surpassed all other metals, Angels and men surpass all the creatures of God. Gold needs the fire and the work of the goldsmith before it can be fashioned into a work of beauty.

Mary, more perfect than all Angels and men, was fashioned by her own will, in the fire of the Holy Spirit, into a thing of the highest beauty. A work of art wrought in gold needs the light to be seen; in the light of the sun, it will be seen in all its perfection. All that the Virgin Mary accomplished, and the beauty of her soul, could not be seen while she was living on earth. Lit by the light of God Himself in heaven, she appeared in the fullness of beauty. All heaven gave praise to her, and to that beauty of soul with which her will had adorned her, a beauty beyond the beauty of all creation, near even to God's own perfection. Mary is enthroned for ever, on that throne placed near to the throne of God.

No one is nearer than she to the Father, the Son and the Holy Spirit. The Father is in the Son, the Son is in the Father, the Holy Spirit is in the Father and the Son. The Son, when He became man in the Virgin's womb, was not thereby divided from the Father and the Holy Spirit. He took our humanity, not losing His Divinity, as Mary acquired Motherhood without loss to her Virginity. God gave to Mary, therefore, a place near to Himself, so that she is ever with the Father, the Son and the Holy Spirit, and ever associated with this Blessed Trinity in all things.

Who could measure the joy in heaven when God raised Mary from this earth? Who will measure our joy when, seeing God face to face, we see too the glory of Mary? The Angels rejoicing in Mary glorify God. The death of Christ has filled again the places made vacant in heaven. The raising of Mary to heaven has increased even the blessedness of heaven. To Adam and Eve, to the Patriarchs and Prophets, to all who died before Christ and were released by His death, to all who have died since Christ's death and been taken to heaven, Mary's entry into heaven is an everlasting joy and delight.

They praise God for her glory, for the honor He has bestowed on her as the one who bore in holiness Christ, their Redeemer and Lord. We may picture the Apostles and many holy ones around Mary as her last hour approached. We know the reverence and honor they paid to her at the moment of her death. We believe that she died, as all others die. We believe that her Son, the Son of God, took her to Himself, and raised her, body and soul, to live for ever in heaven.

Book 11 – Chapter 21
Saturday – Third Reading

The Son of God, the Son of Mary, Christ who is Truth itself, has said to us – return not evil for evil, but return good for evil. Will not He Himself therefore, for He is God, return good for good, and five great reward even for little? He promises in the Gospel that for every good work He will repay a hundredfold. What then will be Mary's reward? Her life was a life of countless good works, a life entirely pleasing to God, a life ever free from defect and unmarred by sin. In all things her will chose, and every member of her body responded gladly to that command. The justice of God has willed that we must rise, body and soul, at the last day, to be repaid for our works.

Body and soul we shall stand before God, for in all things, body and soul act as one. Christ's sinless body rose from the dead, and is now and for ever united in glory with His Divinity. The sinless body of Mary, together with her soul, was taken up by God after her death into heaven, and she is honored there, body and soul, for ever. No mind of ours can comprehend the perfection and glory which is Christ's as reward for His sufferings. No mind of ours can comprehend the glory which is Mary's, in body and soul, for her perfect obedience to God.
The holiness of Mary, those virtues adorning her soul, glorified God her Creator, and she is crowned now in heaven with His reward for those virtues.

The good works of Mary, accomplished by her perfect subjection of body to soul, proclaim for ever her praise. She has done all things as God willed, and omitted nothing that God desired, to win an eternal heavenly glory of both body and soul. No soul, except Christ's, was so filled with holiness and merit as the pure soul of Mary. No body, except the sacred body of her Son, was so worthy to be glorified for its purity and perfection as the pure body of Mary. The justice of God flashed forth when He drove Adam from the garden of Paradise for tasting the forbidden fruit of the tree of knowledge. The mercy of God entered sweetly into this world when the Virgin Mary was born, whom we may fittingly name the tree of life.

The justice of God drove out Adam and Eve into instant exile and misery, for their disobeying. The mercy of God gently invites and attracts to the glory of heaven, all who seek life in obeying. Mary, the tree of life, grew up in this world, to the joy of the Angels in heaven. They longed for the fruit of this tree, which was Christ, and they rejoiced, as they rejoiced in their own eternal happiness, that the great love of God would be made known among men, and their own heavenly ranks increased in number.

The Angel Gabriel rejoiced to be sent with God's message to Mary, and his greeting was spoken with great love for her. When Mary, in the perfection of her holiness and humility, assented, he rejoiced still more that the desire of all the Angels was soon to be fulfilled. We believe and we know, that Mary was assumed body and soul into heaven. We and all our race should ever think of her, and pray to her. In the trials and sorrows of our days, in the sinfulness of our hearts, in the bitterness of life, overshadowed by the certain approach of death. we should look to her, and draw near to her with true sorrow for sin.

We have called her the tree of life. To taste the fruit of the tree, we must first part its branches, and stretch out our hands through the leaves. The tree of life is Mary, the sweet fruit of this tree, Christ her Son. We reach through the branches to pluck the fruit when we greet Mary, as Gabriel did, with great love. She offers us her sweet fruit to taste when she sees our hearts no longer in sin, but willing in all things the will of God. Her intercession and prayer help us to receive the most holy Body of Christ, consecrated for us by the hands of men. This is the Food of true Life, the bread of Angels, and the nourishment of sinful men.

We, though we are sinful and sinning – we are the desire of Christ. His own blood has redeemed us, and He has destined us for heaven, to increase there the numbers of His loved ones. With wise thought, therefore, and with care, with all reverence and love, take Him and eat. Let Christ fulfill in you this desire of His heart.

May the wondrous intercession of the Virgin whose name is Mary win for you this joy from her Son, Jesus Christ, who, with the Father and the Holy Spirit, lives and reigns, God for ever. Amen.

2. Book 12: "Four Prayers"

The prayers written below were divinely revealed to St. Bridget of Sweden.

Since blessed Bridget always petitioned and asked God to pour into her some acceptable manner of praying, it happened one day, while she was praying, that in a wonderful manner she was lifted up in spirit by an elevation of mind. And then were poured into her from God certain most beautiful prayers concerning the life and passion and praise of Christ and concerning the life, compassion, and praise of the most Blessed Virgin Mary.

Afterward she so kept them in memory that every day she would read them devoutly. Wherefore the Blessed Virgin Mary, on a later occasion appearing to her at prayer, said: "I merited for you those prayers. Therefore, when you read them devoutly, you shall be visited with the consolation of my Son."

In this prayer revealed by God to blessed Bridget, the glorious Virgin Mary is devoutly and beautifully praised for her holy conception and infancy, for all her virtuous acts and labors, for the great sorrows of her whole life, for her most holy death and assumption, etc.

Book 12 – Prayer 1

Blessed and revered may you be, my Lady, O Virgin Mary, most holy Mother of God. You are, in truth, His best creation; and no one has ever loved Him so intimately as you, O glorious Lady. Glory be to you, my Lady, O Virgin Mary, Mother of God. That same angel by whom Christ was announced to you announced you yourself to your own father and mother; and of their honest wedlock you were conceived and begotten.

Blessed may you be, my Lady, O Virgin Mary. In your most holy infancy, immediately after your weaning, you were borne by your parents to the temple of God and were, with other virgins, entrusted to the keeping of the devout high priest.

Praise be to you, my Lady, O Virgin Mary. When you reached that age at which you understood that God was your Creator, you forthwith began to love Him intimately above all things. Then too you most discreetly ordered your time, both day and night, by means of various offices and exercises in honor of God. Your sleep, too, and the food for your glorious body were so temperately regulated by you that you were always fit for God's service.

Infinite glory be to you, my Lady, O Virgin Mary, who humbly vowed your virginity to God Himself and therefore had no concern about who would betroth you, for you knew that He to whom you had first given your faith was more mighty and more good than all others combined.

Blessed may you be, my Lady, O Virgin Mary. You were alone and ablaze with ardent love for God and – all your mind and all the strength of your powers being lifted up – you were, with ardor and diligence, contemplating the most high God to whom you had offered your virginity, when the angel was sent to you from God and, in greeting you, announced to you God's will. To him you replied most humbly, professing yourself God's handmaid; and then and there the Holy Spirit wonderfully filled you with all power and virtue. To you, God the Father sent His co-eternal and coequal Son, who came into you then and, of your flesh and blood, took for Himself a human body. Thus, at that blessed hour, the Son of God became, in you, your son, alive in His every limb and without loss of His divine majesty.

Blessed may you be, my Lady, O Virgin Mary. Of your own blessed body, the body of Christ had now been created; and in your womb, you felt His body ever growing and moving even to the time of His glorious nativity. Before anyone else, you yourself touched Him with your holy hands; you wrapped Him in cloths; and, in accord with the prophet's oracle, you laid Him in a manger. With exultant joy, in motherly fashion, you used the most sacred milk of your breasts to nurture Him.

Glory be to you, O my Lady, O Virgin Mary. While still dwelling in a contemptible house, i.e., the stable, you saw mighty kings coming to your Son from afar and humbly offering to Him, with the greatest reverence, their royal guest-gifts. Afterward, with your own precious hands, you presented Him in the temple; and, in your blessed heart, you diligently preserved all that you heard from Him or saw during His infancy.

Blessed may you be, my Lady, O Virgin Mary. With your most holy offspring, you fled into Egypt; and afterward, in joy, you bore Him back to Nazareth. During His physical growth, you saw Him, your Son, humble and obedient to yourself and to Joseph. Blessed may you be, O Lady Virgin Mary. You saw your Son preaching, doing miracles, and choosing the apostles, who, being enlightened by His examples, His miracles, and His teachings, became witnesses of truth that your Jesus is also truly the Son of God: publishing to all nations that it was He who, through Himself, had fulfilled the writings of the prophets when on behalf of the human race He had patiently endured a most hard death.

Blessed may you be, my Lady, O Virgin Mary, who knew beforehand that your Son must be made captive. Later your blessed eyes with sorrow saw Him bound and scourged and crowned with thorns and fixed naked to the cross with nails. You saw many despising Him and calling Him a traitor.

Honor be to you, my Lady, O Virgin Mary. In sorrow, you gazed at your Son as He spoke to you from the cross; and with your blessed ears, you dolefully heard Him, in the agony of death, crying to the Father and commending His own soul into His hands.

Praise be to you, my Lady, O Virgin Mary. With bitter sorrow, you saw your Son hanging on the cross: from the top of His head to the soles of His feet, all black and blue and marked with the red of His own blood, and so cruelly dead. You also gazed at the bitter sight of the holes – in His feet, in His hands, and even in His glorious side. You gazed at His skin, all lacerated without any mercy.

Blessed may you be, my Lady, O Virgin Mary. With tears in your eyes, you saw your Son taken down, wrapped in cloths, buried in a monument, and there guarded by soldiers.
Blessed may you be, my Lady, O Virgin Mary. To the grave intensification of your heart's deep sorrow, you parted from the sepulcher of your Son and, all full of grief, were brought by His friends to the house of John. But there, at once, you felt a relief of your great sorrow because you most surely foreknew that your Son would quickly rise.

Rejoice, my most worthy Lady, O Virgin Mary, for in the same instant that your Son arose from death He willed to make this same fact known to you, His most Blessed Mother. Then and there He appeared to you by Himself, and later He showed to other persons that He was the one who had been raised from death after having endured death in His own living body.

Rejoice therefore, my most worthy Lady, O Virgin Mary. When death had been conquered and death's instigator had been overthrown, and heaven's entry had been opened wide through your Son, you saw Him rising and triumphant with the crown of victory. And on the fortieth day after His resurrection, you saw Him, in the sight of many, ascend with honor to His kingdom in heaven as Himself a king accompanied by angels.

Exult, my most worthy Lady, O Virgin Mary. You merited to see how, after His ascension, your Son suddenly transmitted to His apostles and disciples the Holy Spirit with which He had previously filled you to the full. By increasing the fervor of their charity and the rightness of their Catholic belief, He wonderfully enlightened their hearts.

Rejoice still more, my Lady, O Virgin Mary; and at your joy, let all the world rejoice. For many years after His ascension your Son permitted you to remain in this world for the consolation of His friends and for the strengthening of the faith, for the relief of the poor and for the sound counseling of the apostles. Then, through your prudent words, your seemly behavior, and your virtuous deeds, your Son converted countless Jews and infidel pagans to the Catholic faith; and by wondrously illuminating them, He enlightened them to confess that you are a virgin-mother and that He, your Son, is God with a true human nature.

Blessed may you be, my Lady, O Virgin Mary. In your ardent charity and maternal love, you unceasingly desired at every moment to come to your so well-loved Son now sitting in heaven. While dwelling in this world and sighing after the things of heaven, you humbly conformed to the will of God; wherefore, by the dictates of divine justice, you ineffably increased your eternal glory. To you, O my Lady, O Virgin Mary, be eternal honor and glory. When it pleased God to rescue you from the exile of this world and to honor your soul in His kingdom forever, He then deigned to announce this to you through His angel; and He willed that your venerable body, when dead, be entombed by His apostles in a sepulcher with all reverence.

Be glad, my Lady, O Virgin Mary. For in that most light death of yours, your soul was embraced by the power of God; and He, as a watchful father, protected it from all adversity. Then it was that God the Father subjected to your power all things created. With honor, God the Son placed you, His most worthy Mother, beside Himself on a most lofty seat. And the Holy Spirit, in bringing you to His glorious kingdom as a virgin betrothed to Himself, did wonderfully exalt you.

Rejoice eternally, my Lady, O Virgin Mary. For some days after your death, your body lay entombed in its sepulcher until, with honor and through the power of God, it stood linked anew to your soul. Exult to the full, O Mother of God, O glorious Lady, O Virgin Mary. You merited to see your body revived after your death and assumed with your soul into heaven amidst honor from the angels. You acknowledged that your glorious Son was God with a human nature; and with exultant joy, you saw that He is the most just judge of all and the rewarder of good works.

Rejoice again, my Lady, O Virgin Mary. For your body's most holy flesh knows that it now exists in heaven as both virgin and mother. It sees itself in no way stained by any mortal or venial crime. No, it knows that it did all the works of virtue with such charity that God, in justice, had to revere it with highest honor. Your flesh then understood that the more ardently that anyone loves God in this world, the nearer to Himself will God place that person in heaven. For it was manifestly clear to the whole court of heaven that no angel and no human loved God with such charity as you did; and therefore it was right and just that with honor God Himself placed you, body and soul, on the highest seat of glory.

Blessed may you be, O my Lady, O Virgin Mary. Every faithful creature praises the Holy Trinity for you because you are the Trinity's most worthy creature. For wretched souls you obtain prompt pardon, and for all sinners you stand forth as a most faithful advocate and proxy. Praised therefore be God, the most high Emperor and Lord, who created you for such great honor that you yourself became both Empress and Lady everlastingly in the kingdom of heaven, forever to reign with Him unto ages of ages. Amen.

This prayer was revealed by God to blessed Bridget. In it, by means of a painstakingly detailed narrative, Christ is beautifully and devoutly praised for His glorious incarnation; for all the actions, labors, and sorrows of His life and of His holy death; for His ascension into heaven; for the sending of the Holy Spirit upon the disciples; etc.

BOOK 12 – PRAYER 2

Blessed may you be, my Lord, my God, and my Love most beloved of my soul: O you who are one God in three Persons. Glory and praise be to you, my Lord Jesus Christ. You were sent by the Father into the body of a virgin; and yet you ever remain with the Father in heaven, while the Father, in His divinity, inseparably remained with you in your human nature in this world.

Honor and glory be to you, my Lord Jesus Christ. After having been conceived by the power of the Holy Spirit, you physically grew in the Virgin's womb; and in it you humbly dwelt until the time of your birth. After your delightful nativity, you deigned to be touched by the most clean hands of your Mother, to be wrapped in cloths, and to be laid in a manger.

Blessed may you be, my Lord Jesus Christ. You willed that your immaculate flesh be circumcised and that you be called Jesus. You willed to be offered by your Mother in the temple. Blessed may you be, my Lord Jesus Christ. You had yourself baptized in the Jordan by your servant John. Blessed may you be, my Lord Jesus Christ. With your bless mouth, you preached to human beings the words of life; and in the sight, through yourself, within your actual presence, you worked many miracles. Blessed may you be, my Lord Jesus Christ. By fulfilling the writings of the prophets, you manifested to the world in a rational way that you are the true God.

Blessing and glory be to you, my Lord Jesus Christ. For forty days, you wonderfully fasted in the desert. You permitted yourself to be tempted by your enemy, the devil, whom – when it so pleased you – you drove from yourself with a single word. Blessed may you be, my Lord Jesus Christ. You foretold your death ahead of time. At the last supper, of material bread you wonderfully consecrated your precious Body and charitably bestowed it on your apostles in memory of your most worthy passion. By washing their feet with your own precious and holy hands, you humbly showed your very great humility.

Honor be to you, my Lord Jesus Christ. In fear of suffering and death, you gave forth from your innocent body blood in place of sweat. Nonetheless, you accomplished for us the redemption that you had willed to perform; and thus you manifestly showed the charity that you had toward the human race.

Glory be to you, my Lord Jesus Christ. Sold by your disciple and bought by the Jews, you were made a captive for our sake. Solely by your word, you cast your enemies to the earth; and then of your own will you gave yourself over as a captive to their unclean an grasping hands.

Blessed may you be, my Lord Jesus Christ. You were led to Caiaphas, and you, who are the Judge of all, humbly permitted yourself to be given over to the judgment of Pilate. Blessed may you be, my Lord Jesus Christ. From Pilate the judge, you were sent to Herod; and you permitted yourself to be mocked and scorned by him; and you consented again to be remitted to that same Pilate as judge.

Glory be to you, my Lord Jesus Christ, for the derision that you endured while you stood invested with purple and crowned with the sharpest thorns. With great patience you endured the spitting on your glorious face, the veiling of your eyes, and, on your cheek and neck, the grave and cutting blows of the deadly hands of the wicked.

Praise be to you, my Lord Jesus Christ. Like an innocent lamb, you most patiently permitted yourself to be tied to the column and monstrously scourged; to be led, all bloody, to Pilate's judgment and there be gazed at.

Blessed may you be, my Lord Jesus Christ. Most patiently, in Pilate's presence, with your own blessed ears you willed to hear abuse and lies hurled at you and the voices of the people asking that the guilty robber be acquitted and that you, the innocent, be condemned.

Honor be to you, my Lord Jesus Christ. With your glorious body covered in gore, the judgment on you was the death of the cross. The cross you bore in pain on your sacred shoulders; and, amidst frenzy, you were led to the place of your passion. Despoiled of your garments, thus you willed to be fixed to the wood of the cross.

Glory unmeasured be to you, my Lord Jesus Christ. For us you humbly endured that the Jews stretched out your venerable hands and feet with rope, that they cruelly fixed them with iron nails to the wood of the cross, that they called you a traitor, that in manifold ways they derided you with unspeakable words while above you was inscribed that title of confusion.

Eternal praise and thanksgiving be to you, my Lord Jesus Christ. With what great meekness you suffered for us such cruel sorrows! On the cross your blessed body was emptied of all its strength; your kindly eyes grew dark; as your blood decreased, a pallor covered all your comely face; your blessed tongue grew swollen, hot, and dry; your mouth dripped from the bitter drink; your hair and beard were filled with blood from the wounds of your most holy head; the bones of your hands, of your feet, and of all your precious body were dislocated from their sockets to your great and intense grief; the veins and nerves of all your blessed body were cruelly broken; you were so monstrously scourged and so injured with painful wounds that your most innocent flesh and skin were all intolerably lacerated. Thus afflicted and aggrieved, you, O my most sweet Lord, stood on the cross, and, with patience and humility, awaited in extreme pain the hour of your death.

Perpetual honor be to you, Lord Jesus Christ. Placed in this your anguish, with your kind and charitable eyes you humbly looked upon your most worthy Mother, who never sinned nor ever gave to the slightest sin any consent. While consoling her who was your own, you committed her to the faithful keeping of your disciple.

Eternal blessing be to you, my Lord Jesus Christ. In the agony of death, you gave to all sinners the hope of forgiveness when, to the robber who had turned to you, you mercifully promised the glory of paradise. Eternal praise be to you, my Lord Jesus Christ, for each and every hour that you endured such great bitterness and anguish on the cross for us sinners. For the most acute pains proceeding from your wounds direly penetrated your happy soul and cruelly passed through your most sacred heart until your heart cracked and you happily sent forth your spirit, and, with bowed head, humbly commended it into the hands of God your Father. Then, having died in the body, you remained there all cold.

Blessed may you be, my Lord Jesus Christ. By your precious blood and by your most sacred death, you redeemed souls and mercifully led them back from exile to eternal life. Blessed may you be, my Lord Jesus Christ. You hung dead on the wood of the cross, and straightway you mightily liberated your friends from the prison of hell. Blessed may you be, my Lord Jesus Christ. For our salvation, you permitted your side and your heart to be perforated with a lance, and from that same side you sent forth, in a rich flow, water and your precious blood in order to redeem us. Before the judge's leave had been given, you willed that your most sacred body not be taken down from the cross.

Glory be to you, my Lord Jesus Christ. You willed that your blessed body be taken down from the cross by your friends and that it be laid in the hands of your most unhappy Mother. You permitted that it be wrapped in cloths by her and be buried in a monument and that it be guarded there by soldiers.

Eternal honor be to you, my Lord Jesus Christ. On the third day, you rose from the dead, and you showed yourself alive to such others as it so pleased you. After forty days, while many watched, you ascended to the heavens; and there, in honor, you placed your friends whom you had delivered from Tartarus [Limbo].

Jubilation and praise eternal be to you, Lord Jesus Christ. You sent the Holy Spirit to the hearts of your disciples; and in their spirits, you immeasurably increased divine love.

Blessed may you be, and praiseworthy and glorious unto the ages, my Lord Jesus. You sit upon the throne in your kingdom of heaven, in the glory of your divinity, corporeally alive, with all your most holy limbs that you took from the flesh of the Virgin. Even thus shall you come on the day of judgment to judge the souls of all the living and the dead: you, who live and reign with the Father and the Holy Spirit unto ages of ages. Amen.

In this prayer, revealed by God to blessed Bridget, praise is given in a beautiful way to all the members of the most holy body of our Lord Jesus Christ and to His body's most virtuous actions.

BOOK 12 – PRAYER 3

My Lord Jesus Christ, although I know well that your blessed body is unceasingly praised and glorified by the harmonious jubilee of the citizens of heaven above, and yet, because I am bound by a debt to render to you infinite thanksgiving, therefore I, although a person unwise and unworthy, desire nevertheless with all my heart and with all my mouth to offer to all the members of your precious body such thanks as I can and praise and honor.

My Lord Jesus Christ, you are truly the High Priest and Pontiff who first and before all others wondrously consecrated of material bread your true and blessed Body that you might satisfy us with the bread of angels. Therefore, may your glorious priestly seat at the right hand of God your Father, in your divinity, be happy and blessed unto eternity. Amen.

My Lord Jesus Christ, you truly are the head of all men and angels, the worthy King of kings and Lord of lords; and you do all your works out of true and ineffable charity. You humbly permitted your blessed head to be crowned with a crown of thorns. Blessed, therefore, be your head and hair; and may they be gloriously adorned with an imperial diadem. May heaven and earth and sea and all things created be subject and obedient to your empire and your power unto eternity. Amen.

My Lord Jesus Christ, your splendid forehead never turned away from right justice and truth. Blessed, therefore, be that same forehead of yours, and, with royal and triumphant glory, may it be perpetually praised by all creatures together. Amen.

My Lord Jesus Christ, with your bright eyes of pity you look kindly upon all who with true charity ask of you grace and mercy. Blessed, therefore, be your eyes, your eyelids, and your glorious eyebrows; and may all your fair and lovely sight be unceasingly glorified by the whole heavenly army of citizens on high. Amen.

My Lord Jesus Christ, with your kindly ears you gladly hear and hearken to all who humbly address you. Blessed, therefore, be those ears of yours; and may they be eternally filled with all honor. Amen.

My Lord Jesus Christ, your most sweet and blessed nostrils did not shrink from the stench of the putrid cadaver of the dead Lazarus or even from the horrid smell that spiritually proceeded from the traitor Judas when he kissed you. Blessed, therefore, be your precious nostrils; and may all expend on them the odor of sweetness and praise forever. Amen.

My Lord Jesus Christ, for our bodily and spiritual health and salvation and for our instruction in faith, you, with your own blessed mouth and lips, very often preached the words of life and of doctrine. Blessed, therefore, be your venerable mouth and your lips for every word that proceeded from them. Amen.

My Lord Jesus Christ, with your most clean teeth, you most moderately chewed physical food for the sustenance of your blessed body. Blessed, therefore, and honored be your teeth by all your creatures. Amen.

My Lord Jesus Christ, your tongue never moved to speak and never kept silence, except with justice and utility and to the extent that such action had been foreordained in your divinity. Blessed, therefore, be that same tongue of yours. Amen.

My Lord Jesus Christ, in accordance with your age, you fittingly wore a fine beard on your handsome face. May your venerable beard, therefore, be everlastingly revered and adored. Amen.

My Lord Jesus Christ, blessed be your throat, your stomach, and your viscera; and may all your sacred inwards be perpetually honored for the fact that they decently nourished your precious body in due order and perfectly sustained your bodily life for the redemption of souls and to the joy of the angels. Amen.

My Lord Jesus Christ, you are worthily called a leader by all because you bore on your holy shoulders and neck the burdensome bulk of the cross before you mightily shattered the gates of hell and led the souls of the elect back to heaven. Therefore, to your blessed neck and shoulders that so endured, be honor and glory eternally without end. Amen.

My Lord Jesus Christ, your blessed, royal, and magnificent heart could never, by torments or terrors or blandishments, be swayed from the defense of your kingdom of truth and justice. You did not spare your most worthy blood in any way; but rather, with your magnificent heart, you faithfully strove for justice and the law and intrepidly preached to your friends and to your enemies the law's precepts and the counsels of perfection. By dying in battle to defend these things, you – and your holy followers with you – have obtained the victory.

Therefore, it is right that your unconquered heart be ever magnified in heaven and on earth and be unceasingly praised with triumphal honor by all creatures and soldiers. Amen.

My Lord Jesus Christ, the strenuous soldiers and faithful servants of this world gladly expose their own lives to death in war in order that their lords may enjoy safety of life; but you, O my good Lord, quickly hastened to the death of the cross in order that your servants might not miserably perish. Wherefore it is just that your glorious and intrepid breast be eternally adored by all your servants, whom you have thus delivered, and by all others and that it be humbly praised even by the angelic choirs. Amen.

My Lord Jesus Christ, with your venerable hands and arms you surpassed the strength of Samson in a wonderful way as you patiently endured that they be fixed to the wood of the cross and thus, with violence, snatched your friends from hell. Therefore to these same limbs of yours, from all whom you have redeemed, may there be shown unceasing reverence, eternal praise, and everlasting glory. Amen.

My Lord Jesus Christ, may your precious ribs and your back be blessed and honored unto eternity by all human beings who sweat over labors spiritual and earthly. For from your infancy even to your death, you labored unceasingly for our redemption; and with great pain and burdensomeness, you bore our sins on your back. Amen.

My Lord Jesus Christ, supreme purity and true cleanness, may your most innocent loins be blessed and praised above all the angels' cleanness which is in heaven and above the purity of all who have preserved their chastity and virginity in the world; for the chastity and virginity of them all cannot be compared to your cleanness and your purity. Amen.

My Lord Jesus Christ, may your knees, with their hams and your shins, be revered and humbly honored by all creatures in heaven and on earth above all who show reverence and honor by kneeling in the presence of their lords and masters; for you, the Lord of all, in all humility knelt before your own disciples. Amen.

My Lord Jesus Christ, good Teacher, may your most blessed feet be blessed and perennially adored; for, in this world, to your great sorrow, you walked with unshod feet along the harsher way that you taught to others, and at the end, for our sake, you permitted them to be fixed with hard nails to the cross

– you who live and reign with God the Father in the unity of the Holy Spirit through all ages of ages. Amen.

In this prayer, which was divinely revealed to blessed Bridget, most devout and beautiful praise is given to all the members of the glorious body of the Virgin Mary and to all her body's virtuous actions.

BOOK 12 – PRAYER 4

O my Lady, my life, O Queen of heaven, O Mother of God, although I am certain that your glorious body is unceasingly praised in heaven with melodious jubilee by all the heavenly court, still I, although an unworthy person, desire with all my heart to render here on earth such praise and thanks as I can to all your precious limbs.

Therefore, O my Lady, O Virgin Mary, praised be your hair with all its strands, now decorated with a diadem of glory; for your hair is brighter than the radiance of the sun. Just as the hairs of the head cannot be computed, even so are your virtues innumerable.

O my Lady, O Virgin Mary, may your forehead and your most honest face be together praised above the whiteness of the moon, for none of the faithful in this dark world ever looked to you without feeling some spiritual consolation poured into Himself at the sight of you. Blessed may you be, my Lady, O Virgin Mary. Your eyebrows and your eyelids exceed in the brightness of their splendor the rays of the sun. Blessed be your most chaste eyes, O my Lady, O Virgin Mary. They coveted none of the transitory things that they saw in this world. As often as you lifted up your eyes, their appearance excelled the splendor of the stars in the sight of the whole heavenly court.

O my Lady, O Virgin Mary, may both your most blessed cheeks be praised above the beauty of the dawn, which so beautifully rises with its colors white and red. Even thus, while you were in the world, did your lovely cheeks shine with bright splendor in the sight of God and the angels because you never displayed them for worldly pomp or vanity.

O my Lady, O Virgin Mary, revered and honored be your most honest ears above all the forces of the sea and above the motion of all the waters; for your ears ever manfully militated against all the unclean flux of worldly hearing. O Virgin Mary, my Mistress, may your most sweet nose glory! By the power of the Holy Spirit, it never drew or sent forth a breath without all your thought being ever in the presence of the most High. Although at times you slept, you never turned your will from Him. Therefore, to that same nose of yours and to your most blessed nostrils be ever given an odor of sweetness, praise, and honor above the mingled odor of all the spices and all the herbs that habitually send forth a delightful fragrance.

O my Lady, O Virgin Mary, praised be your tongue – so pleasing to God and to the angels – above all fruitful trees. Every word that your tongue uttered never harmed any person but always came forth to someone's advantage. Your tongue was very prudent, and all found it sweeter to hear than the sweetest fruit is sweet to taste. O my Queen and my Lady, O Virgin Mary, may your blessed mouth and your lips be praised above the loveliness of roses and all other flowers and especially for that your blessed and most humble word in which, with this same precious mouth of yours, you responded to God's angel when through you God willed to fulfill in the world His will, which He had foretold through the prophets. By virtue of that word, you diminished the power of the demons in hell and honorably restored the choirs of angels in heaven.

O Virgin Mary, my Lady and my consolation, may your neck, your shoulders, and your back be perpetually honored above the charm of all lilies, for you never bent these members of yours and never straightened them again, except for some useful purpose or for the honor of God. Just as the lily moves and bends at the blowing of the winds, so all your members moved at the infusion of the Holy Spirit. O my Lady, my strength and my sweetness, may your most holy arms, your hands, and your fingers be blessed and eternally honored above all precious gems, which are comparable to your virtuous works. Just as your virtuous works allured the Son of God to you, even so did your arms and hands sweetly bind Him in a maternal embrace of love.

O my Lady and my enlightenment, blessed be your most sacred breasts above all the sweetest springs of healing waters. Just as their welling water supplies solace and refreshment for the thirsty, your sacred breasts, in giving milk to the Son of God, supplied us in our need with medicine and consolation.

O my Lady, O Virgin Mary, blessed be your most precious bosom above the purest gold. When you stood all sorrowful beneath the cross of your Son, then – at the sound of the hammers – you felt your glorious bosom most sharply constricted as if in a hard press. Although you heartily loved your Son, you nevertheless preferred Him to endure that most bitter punishment in order that He might die for the redemption of souls, rather than that He avoid this death to their loss. Thus too did you stand most firm in the virtue of constancy when in every adversity you totally conformed yourself to the divine will.

O my Lady, O joy of my heart, O Virgin Mary, may your most venerable heart be glorified and revered. It was so afire for the honor of God – more so than all other creatures of heaven and earth – that the flame of its charity ascended the heights of heaven to God the Father, and, because of this, God's Son descended from the Father into your glorious womb with the fervor of the Holy Spirit. Nevertheless, the Son was not separated from the Father even though, in accordance with the Father's plan, He was most honestly made human in your virginal womb.

O my Lady, most fertile and most virginal Virgin Mary, blessed be your most blessed womb above all fruitfully sprouting fields. Just as the seed that has fallen upon good ground brings forth for its owner fruit a hundredfold, even so your womb, a virgin-womb and yet most fertile, brought forth for God the Father blessed fruit, more than a thousandfold. Just as the lord of a field glories in its fertile abundance of fruit and just as the little birds and the animals feed in it with delight, even so did the blessed and fertile fruit of the little field of your womb cause high honor for God in heaven, rejoicing for the angels, and, for humans on earth, a lavish flow of sustenance and life.

O my Lady, Virgin most prudent, may your most sacred feet be eternally praised above all roots that unceasingly bear fruit. May your feet be thus blessed because they carried the glorious Son of God enclosed in your body as its sweetest fruit while your body itself was inviolate and your virginity remained uninjured forever. Oh with what honesty your most sacred feet went their way! Truly, at each of their prints, the King of heaven stood consoled and all the court of heaven rejoiced and was very glad.

O my Lady, O Virgin Mary, O Mother of all, may God the Father, together with the Son and the Holy Spirit, be eternally praised in His incomprehensible majesty for that most sacred cell of your whole body in which God's Son so sweetly rested – He whom the whole army of angels praises in heaven and whom the whole Church reverently adores on earth.

And you, my Lord, my King, and my God, to you be perpetual honor, perennial praise, blessing, and glory, and infinite thanksgiving. For you created this Virgin so worthy and so honest; and you chose her for yourself as your Mother for the sake of all who in any way have been consoled in heaven and on earth and for the sake of those in purgatory who have had, through her, assistance and solace. You live and reign with God the Father in the unity of the Holy Spirit, one God, through all ages of ages. Amen.

3. The Fifteen Prayers of Saint Bridget to our Suffering Lord Jesus Christ

For a long time, St. Bridget wanted to know the number of wounds Our Lord received during His Passion. He one day appeared to her and said, "I received 5480 blows on My Body. If you wish to honor them in some way, say 15 Our Fathers and 15 Hail Marys with the following Prayers (which He taught her) for a whole year. When the year is up, you will have honored each one of My Wounds."

First Prayer
1 Our Father... (Our Father, Who art in heaven, Hallowed be Thy Name. Thy Kingdom come. Thy Will be done, on earth as it is in Heaven. Give us this day our daily bread. And forgive us our trespasses, as we forgive those who trespass against us. And lead us not into temptation, but deliver us from evil. Amen.)
1 Hail Mary... (Hail Mary, Full of Grace, The Lord is with thee. Blessed art thou among women, and blessed is the fruit of thy womb, Jesus. Holy Mary, Mother of God, pray for us sinners now, and at the hour of death. Amen.)
O Jesus Christ! Eternal Sweetness to those who love You; Joy surpassing all joy and all desire; Salvation and Hope of all sinners, Who proved that You have no greater desire than to be among men, even assuming human nature at the fullness of time for the love of men; recall all the sufferings You endured from the instant of Your Conception and especially during Your Passion, as it was decreed and ordained from all Eternity in the Divine Plan. Remember, O Lord, that during the Last Supper with Your disciples, having washed their feet, You gave them Your Most Precious Body and Blood, and while at the same time You sweetly consoled them, You foretold to them Your coming Passion. Remember the sadness and bitterness which You experienced in Your Soul as You Yourself bore witness saying, "My soul is sorrowful even unto death." Remember the fear, anguish and pain that You suffered in Your delicate Body before the torment of the Crucifixion, when, after having prayed three times, bathed in a sweat of blood, You were betrayed by Judas, Your disciple;. arrested by the people of a nation You had chosen and elevated; accused by false witnesses; unjustly judged by three judges during the flower of Your youth and during the solemn Paschal Season. Remember that You were despoiled of Your garments and clothed in those of derision; that Your Face and Eyes were veiled. That You were struck, crowned with thorns and a reed placed in Your Hands; that You were crushed with blows and overwhelmed with insults and outrages. In

memory of all these pains and sufferings which You endured before Your Passion on the Cross, grant me before my death true contrition, a sincere and entire confession, worthy satisfaction and the remission of all my sins. Amen.

Second Prayer
1 Our Father...
1 Hail Mary...
O Jesus! True liberty of Angels, paradise of delights, remember the horror and sadness which You endured when Your enemies, like furious lions, surrounded You and by thousands of insults, spitting, blows, lacerations and other unheard of cruelties, tormented You at will. In consideration of these torments and insulting words, I beseech You, O My Savior, to deliver me from all my enemies, visible and invisible and to bring me under Your Protection to the perfection of eternal salvation.
Amen.

Third Prayer
1 Our Father...
1 Hail Mary...
O Jesus! Creator of Heaven and earth. Whom nothing can encompass or limit. You who enfold and hold all under Your Loving Power, remember the very bitter pain You suffered when the Jews nailed Your Sacred Hands and Feet to the Cross by blow after blow with big blunt nails and not finding You in a pitiable enough state to satisfy their rage, they enlarged Your Wounds and added pain to pain and with indescribable cruelty stretched Your Body on the Cross, pulled You from all sides, thus dislocating Your Limbs. I beg of You, O Jesus, by the memory of this most Loving Suffering of the Cross, to grant me the Grace to fear You and to love You. Amen.

Fourth Prayer
1 Our Father...
1 Hail Mary...
O Jesus! Heavenly Physician, raised aloft on the Cross to heal our wounds with Yours. Remember the bruises which You suffered and the weakness of all Your Members which were distended to such a degree that never was there pain like unto Yours. From the crown of Your Head to the soles of Your feet there was not one spot on Your Body that was not in torment, and yet, forgetting all Your sufferings, You did not cease to pray to Your Heavenly Father for Your enemies saying, "Father, forgive them, for they know not what they do." Through this Great Mercy and in memory of this suffering, grant that the remembrance of Your Most Bitter Passion may effect in us a perfect contrition and the remission of all our sins. Amen.

Fifth Prayer
1 Our Father...
1 Hail Mary...
O Jesus! Mirror of Eternal Splendor, remember the sadness which You experienced when, contemplating in the Light of Your Divinity the predestination of those who would be saved by the Merits of Your Sacred Passion, You saw at the same time the great multitude of reprobates who would be damned for their sins, and You complained bitterly of those hopeless lost and unfortunate sinners. Through this Abyss of Compassion and Pity, and especially through the Goodness which You displayed to the good thief when You said to him, "This day, you shall be with Me in Paradise," I beg of You, O Sweet Jesus, that at the hour of my death, You will show me Mercy. Amen.

Sixth Prayer
1 Our Father...
1 Hail Mary...
O Jesus! Beloved and Most Desirable King, remember the grief You suffered, when naked and like a common criminal, You were fastened and raised on the Cross. When all Your friends abandoned You, except Your Beloved Mother, who remained close to You during Your Agony and whom You entrusted to Your faithful disciple when You said to Mary, "Woman, behold your son!" and to St. John, "Behold your Mother!" I beg of You, O My Savior, by the sword of sorrow which pierced the soul of Your Holy Mother, to have compassion on me in all my trials and tribulations, both corporal and spiritual, and to assist me in all my trials, and especially at the hour of my death. Amen

Seventh Prayer
1 Our Father...
1 Hail Mary...
O Jesus! Inexhaustible Fountain of Compassion, Who by a profound gesture of Love, said from the Cross, "I thirst!" suffered from the thirst for the salvation of the human race, I beg of You, O My Savior, to inflame in our hearts the desire to tend toward perfection in all our acts and to extinguish in us the concupiscence of the flesh and the ardor of worldly desires. Amen.

Eighth Prayer
1 Our Father...
1 Hail Mary...
O Jesus! Sweetness of Hearts, Delight of The Spirit, by the bitterness of the vinegar and gall which You tasted on the Cross for Love of us, grant us the grace to receive worthily Your Precious Body and Blood during our life and at

the hour of our death, that they may serve as a remedy and consolation for our souls. Amen.

Ninth Prayer
1 Our Father...
1 Hail Mary...
O Jesus! Royal Virtue, Joy of the Mind, recall the pain You endured when, plunged in an ocean of bitterness at the approach of death, insulted, outraged by the Jews, You cried out in a loud voice that You were abandoned by Your Father, saying, "My God, My God, why have You forsaken Me?" Through this anguish, I beg of You, O My Savior, not to abandon me in the terrors and pains of my death. Amen.

Tenth Prayer
1 Our Father...
1 Hail Mary...
O Jesus! Who are the beginning and end of all things, life and virtue, remember that for our sakes You were plunged in an abyss of suffering from the soles of Your feet to the Crown of Your Head. In consideration of the enormity of Your Wounds, teach me to keep, through pure love, Your Commandments, whose way is wide and easy for those who love You.
Amen.

Eleventh Prayer
1 Our Father...
1 Hail Mary...
O Jesus! Deep Abyss of Mercy. I beg of You, in memory of Your Wounds which penetrated to the very marrow of Your Bones and to the depths of Your Being, to draw me, a miserable sinner, overwhelmed by my offenses, away from sin and to hide me in Your Wounds until Your anger and just indignation shall have passed away. Amen.

Twelfth Prayer
1 Our Father...
1 Hail Mary...
O Jesus! Mirror of Truth, Symbol of Unity, Link of Charity, remember the multitude of wounds with which You were covered from head to foot, torn and reddened by the spilling of Your adorable Blood. O great and universal pain which You suffered in Your Virginal Flesh for the love of us! Sweetest Jesus! What is there that You could have done for us that You have not done?! May the Fruit of Your Sufferings be renewed in my soul by the faithful remembrance of Your Passion, and may Your Love increase in my heart each day until I see You

in eternity; You who are the treasury of every real good and every joy, which I beg You to grant me, O Sweetest Jesus, in Heaven. Amen.

Thirteenth Prayer
1 Our Father...
1 Hail Mary...
O Jesus! Strong Lion, Immortal and Invincible King, remember the pain which You endured when, all Your Strength, both moral and physical, was entirely exhausted, You bowed Your Head saying, "It is accomplished!" Through this anguish and grief, I beg of You Lord Jesus, to have mercy on me at the hour of my death when my mind will be greatly troubled and my soul will be in anguish. Amen.

Fourteenth Prayer
1 Our Father...
1 Hail Mary...
O Jesus! Only Son of the Father, Splendor and Figure of His Substance, remember the simple and humble recommendation You made of Your Soul to Your Heavenly Father saying, "Father, into Your Hands I commend My Spirit!" And with Your Body all torn, Your Heart broken and the Bowels of Your Mercy open to redeem us, You expired. By this Precious Death, I beg of You, O King of Saints, comfort me and help me to resist the devil, the flesh and the world, so that being dead to the world, I may live to You alone. I beg of You, at the hour of my death, to receive me, a pilgrim and an exile returning to You. Amen.

Fifteenth Prayer
1 Our Father...
1 Hail Mary...
O Jesus! True and Fruitful Vine, remember the abundant outpouring of Blood which You so generously shed from Your Sacred Body as juice from grapes in a wine press. From Your Side, pierced with a lance by a soldier, Blood and Water issued forth until there was not left in Your Body a single drop, and finally, like a bundle of myrrh, lifted to the top of the Cross, Your delicate Flesh was destroyed, the very substance of Your Body withered and the marrow of Your Bones dried up. Through this bitter Passion and through the outpouring of Your Precious Blood, I beg of You, O Sweet Jesus, to receive my soul when I am in my death agony. Amen.

Conclusion
O Sweet Jesus! Pierce my heart so that my tears of penitence will be my bread day and night. May I be converted entirely to You. May my heart be Your perpetual habitation. May my conversation be pleasing to You and may the end

of my life be so praiseworthy, that I may merit Heaven and there with Your saints, praise You forever. Amen.

Made in the USA
Monee, IL
01 February 2023